# Earth Song

words and music by **Susan Reed**

art by **Mariona Cabassa**

**Barefoot Books**

*step inside a story*

The earth circles round the sun each year.
Past days, weeks, and months, our birthdays we cheer,

growing taller, faster, smarter, wiser.
**The earth circles round the sun each year.**

And the stars shine from the heavens,
reaching as far, as far as can be.

And the stars shine from the heavens,
**the earth circles round the sun each year.**

The earth, she tilts and makes the seasons.
When we're tilting towards the sun, our summer has begun.

When we're leaning away, winter's frost is on its way.

**The earth, she tilts and makes the seasons.**

And the stars shine from the heavens,
reaching as far, as far as can be.

And the stars shine from the heavens,

**the earth, she tilts and makes the seasons.**

We have one moon; it circles thirteen times a year.
We all know the same moon and hold it dear.

No matter where your home lies,
in peace we share the moon.

The moon circles thirteen times a year.

And the stars shine from the heavens,
reaching as far, as far as can be.

And the stars shine from the heavens,
the moon circles thirteen times a year.

The earth spins round, turning daytime into night.
We don't feel the turning, but the yearning at the sight

of the sun rising, as we start each day anew.
**The earth spins daytime into night.**

And the stars shine from the heavens,

reaching as far, as far as can be.

And the stars shine from the heavens,
the earth spins daytime into night.
**The earth spins daytime into night.**

# What does the earth do?

## Circles round the sun each year

The earth is constantly moving around the sun in a path called an **orbit**. Each time earth completes one full orbit, a year has passed!

## Tilts and makes the seasons

As the earth travels around, it is slightly tilted. As it spins, different parts get varying amounts of sunlight. When the part of the earth you're living on is tilted away from the sun, it is winter. When the part of the earth you're living on is tilted towards the sun, it is summer. Summer sun shines more directly at us, and the days are longer. These direct summer sun rays are hotter than winter rays, and the long hours of sunlight give earth plenty of time to heat up.

# Spins daytime into night

When the earth moves, it is also spinning on its **axis** (an imaginary straight line that objects rotate around). The side of the earth that is facing the sun is in the light and we call that daytime. The side of earth facing away from the sun is in the dark and we call that nighttime.

axis

orbit

# What is the earth?

Our home, the earth, is just one of eight planets in our solar system. It's the third closest planet to the sun and the only place in the universe (that we know of!) that has life.

# What is the sun?

The sun is actually a star, like the other stars we see glittering in the night sky. It seems bigger than all the others because we are so much closer to it! Like all stars, the sun is a massive ball of really hot gas. And even though the sun looks small from our windows, it's actually a million times larger than the earth.

# Our moon circles thirteen times a year

Just like the earth is constantly spinning in a circle around the sun, the moon is constantly moving in a circle around the earth. This path is called the lunar orbit and it takes the moon 27 days to complete. This means it will circle the earth 13 times each year.

## The phases of the moon

If you look up at the night sky every night for a month, you'll notice how the moon's shape seems to change! Depending on where the moon is in its orbit around the earth, sometimes the side we see is fully lit in a full moon, sometimes partially lit in a crescent moon, and sometimes not lit at all in a new moon.

# What is a moon?

A moon is a **natural satellite** — an object that orbits a planet. Earth only has one moon, but other planets in our solar system have lots more. Saturn has at least 146! The first person to walk on the moon was the American astronaut Neil Armstrong in 1969.

## How do the earth and the moon stay in orbit?

The earth and moon move because of a force called **gravity** that pulls things towards each other. Bigger objects have more gravity. The sun is very big and has a lot of gravity, so it keeps the earth and the other planets in our solar system circling around it. Similarly, the earth has strong gravity that keeps the moon going around it. The moon has gravity too, which pulls on the water in our oceans and creates the rhythm of tides felt around the world.

# Earth Song

To my husband Ken and my children: Jon, Kate, and Allie.
I love your questions about our place in space! – S. R.

To Baba – M. C.

Barefoot Books
23 Bradford Street, 2nd Floor
Concord, MA 01742

Barefoot Books
29/30 Fitzroy Square
London, W1T 6LQ

Reproduction by Bright Arts, Hong Kong
Printed in China
This book was typeset in Balsamiq Sans and Kids Rock
The illustrations were prepared in gouache, crayons,
wax crayons, and digital methods

Hardback ISBN 979-8-88859-222-9
Paperback ISBN 979-8-88859-223-6
E-book ISBN 979-8-88859-296-0

British Cataloguing-in-Publication Data:
a catalogue record for this book is available from the British Library

Library of Congress Cataloging-in-Publication Data
is available under LCCN 2024932068

1 3 5 7 9 8 6 4 2

Banjo, guitar, vocals by Susan Reed, bass by Domenick Fiore, and
back up vocals by Emily Collins, Jen Collins, Deb Dunham,
Grace Dunham, Harper Mills, Allie Reed, and Kate Reed
Musical arrangement ℗ 2024 by Susan Reed
Produced, mixed, and mastered by Susan Reed
Animation by Collaborate Agency, UK

First published in the United States of America by Barefoot Books, Inc
and in Great Britain by Barefoot Books, Ltd in 2024
Graphic design by Lindsey Leigh, Barefoot Books
Edited and art directed by Erin Lueck, Barefoot Books

Go to *www.barefootbooks.com/earthsong* to access
your audio singalong and video animation online.